Frugal Living for Beginners

Identifying areas for potential savings

By

Lorenzo Zayne

Table of Contents

CHAPTER 1

Introduction to Frugal Living

So, you're interested in frugal living, huh? Maybe you've heard the term thrown around and wondered what all the fuss is about. Or perhaps you're feeling the pinch in your wallet and looking for ways to stretch your hard-earned cash a bit further. Whatever brought you here, you're in for a treat. Let's break down this whole frugal living thing and see if it might be a good fit for you.

1.1 What is frugal living?

First things first – what exactly do we mean when we talk about frugal living? Well, at its core, frugal living is all about being smart with your money and resources. It's not about being cheap or miserly (we'll get to that misconception later), but rather about making conscious choices to live within or below your means.

Think of frugal living as a mindset. It's about prioritizing what truly matters to you and cutting back on the stuff that doesn't. It's like Marie Kondo-ing your finances – keeping what sparks joy and ditching the rest. Frugal folks are always on the lookout for ways to save money without sacrificing their quality of life.

Now, this doesn't mean you have to start dumpster diving or wearing clothes with holes in them (unless that's your thing, no judgment here). Frugal living can look different for everyone. For some, it might mean cooking at home more often instead of eating out. For others, it could be about finding creative ways to have fun without spending a ton of cash.

The key is to be intentional with your spending. Before you whip out that credit card, a frugal person might ask themselves: "Do I really need this? Is there a cheaper alternative? Could I borrow or rent this instead of buying it?" It's about being mindful of where your money's going and making sure it aligns with your values and goals.

Frugal living also often goes hand in hand with sustainability. When you're trying to stretch your dollars, you naturally tend to waste less, reuse more, and think twice before buying new stuff. So not only is it good for your wallet, but it can be pretty great for the planet too.

1.2 Benefits of adopting a frugal lifestyle

Now that we've got a handle on what frugal living is, let's talk about why you might want to give it a shot. Trust me, the benefits go way beyond just having a few extra bucks in your pocket (although that's pretty sweet too).

First off, the most obvious benefit: you'll save money. I know, shocking, right? But seriously, when you start being more intentional about your spending, you'd be amazed at how much you can save. Those little expenses that seem harmless – the daily coffee run, the impulse buy at the checkout counter – they add up fast. Cut those out, and suddenly you've got a nice little chunk of change to play with.

But here's where it gets really cool: frugal living can give you freedom. Yeah, you heard me right. Freedom. When you're not constantly stressed about money, when you're not living paycheck to paycheck, you have more options. Maybe you can finally afford to take that dream vacation, or maybe you can start saving for a down payment on a house. Heck, maybe you can even retire early if that's your jam.

Frugal living can also lead to less stress. Money worries are a huge source of anxiety for a lot of people. When you're living frugally, you're more likely to have an emergency fund tucked away. So when life throws you a curveball (and let's face it, it always does), you're better prepared to handle it without freaking out.

Another cool benefit? You might find yourself becoming more creative and resourceful. When you're trying to save money, you start looking at things differently. Maybe instead of buying a new piece of furniture, you learn how to upcycle an old one. Or instead of paying for expensive entertainment, you discover a hidden talent for DIY projects. Frugal living can push you out of your comfort zone in the best possible way.

And let's not forget about the environmental impact. Like I mentioned earlier, frugal living often goes hand in hand with being more eco-friendly. You might find yourself reducing waste, consuming less, and generally living a more sustainable lifestyle. It feels pretty good to know you're doing your part for the planet while also saving some cash.

frugal living can help you appreciate what you have more. When you're not constantly chasing the next big purchase or trying to keep up with the Joneses, you start to focus on what really matters. You might find more joy in experiences rather than things, or discover that the best things in life really are free (or at least pretty darn cheap).

CHAPTER 2

Assessing Your Current Financial Situation

You know that feeling when you're about to check your bank account after a weekend of fun? That little twinge of anxiety? Well, we're going to face that head-on, but I promise it'll be worth it. Understanding where you're at financially is like having a map before starting a road trip. Sure, you could just start driving and hope for the best, but wouldn't it be better to know exactly where you are and where you're headed?

2.1 Tracking expenses

First things first – we need to figure out where your money's actually going. It's easy to think we know, but trust me, most of us are way off when we try to estimate our spending. I remember when

I first started tracking my expenses, I was shocked to discover how much I was spending on random snacks and coffees throughout the month. It was like my money was evaporating into thin air!

So, how do we track expenses? There are a few ways you can go about this:

1. The old-school method: Get yourself a little notebook and pen, and write down every single thing you spend money on for a month. And I mean everything – from your rent or mortgage payment down to that pack of gum you bought on a whim. It might seem tedious, but it's a great way to really connect with your spending habits.

2. The spreadsheet approach: If you're more of a digital person, set up a simple spreadsheet. You can create categories like "Housing," "Transportation,"

"Food," "Entertainment," etc., and log your expenses daily or weekly.

3. The app route: There are tons of great apps out there that can help you track your spending. Some even link to your bank accounts and credit cards to automatically categorize your expenses. Personal favorites include Mint, YNAB (You Need A Budget), and Personal Capital, but there are loads to choose from.

Whichever method you choose, the key is to be consistent and honest. No judgment here – we're just trying to get an accurate picture of where your money's going. Try to track for at least a month to get a good sense of your spending patterns.

Now, as you're tracking, you might start to notice some patterns. Maybe you're spending way more on eating out than you realized, or perhaps your online shopping habit is a bit more intense than you thought. That's okay! The point isn't to beat yourself up, but to bring awareness to your spending habits.

One thing that really helped me when I started tracking was to look at my expenses in terms of hours worked. Like, that new shirt I bought on impulse? That was two hours of work at my job. Suddenly, I started asking myself if each purchase was really worth the time I spent earning that money. It's a great way to put your spending into perspective.

2.2 Creating a budget

Alright, now that we've got a handle on where your money's going, it's time to create a budget. I know, I know – the word "budget" sounds about as fun as a root canal. But hear me out: a budget isn't about restricting yourself. It's about giving yourself permission to spend on the things that really matter to you.

Think of a budget like a spending plan. It's you telling your money where to go, instead of wondering where it went. Here's how to get started:

1. List your income: Start with your take-home pay. If you have a variable income, use an average month or your lowest month as a baseline.

2. List your fixed expenses: These are the bills that stay pretty much the same each month – things like rent/mortgage, car payments, insurance, etc.

3. List your variable expenses: This is where your expense tracking comes in handy. Look at categories like groceries, entertainment, clothing, etc.

4. Set spending limits: Based on your income and your tracked expenses, set realistic limits for each category. The key word here is realistic. If you're currently spending $500 a month on groceries, it's probably not realistic to suddenly cut that to $100. Start with small, achievable cuts.

5. Don't forget savings: Aim to put something aside for savings, even if it's just a small amount to start. paying yourself first is a key principle of good financial health.

There are different budgeting methods out there, and you might need to experiment to find what works best for you. Here are a few popular ones:

- The 50/30/20 budget: 50% of your income goes to needs, 30% to wants, and 20% to savings and debt repayment.

- Zero-based budgeting: Every dollar gets a job. You allocate all of your income to expenses, savings, and debt payments until you reach zero.

- The envelope system: You use actual cash in envelopes for different spending categories. When the envelope's empty, that's it for the month.

Personally, I'm a fan of a modified zero-based budget. I like knowing where every dollar is going, but I also keep a small "miscellaneous" category for those unexpected expenses that always seem to pop up.

Your budget isn't set in stone. Life happens, priorities change, and that's okay. The important thing is to stay flexible and adjust as needed. Maybe one month you need to spend more on car repairs, so you cut back a bit on entertainment. It's all about balance and making conscious choices.

One tip that's really helped me stick to my budget is to check in with it regularly. I have a weekly "money date" with myself where I review my spending, make sure I'm on track, and adjust if needed. It might sound a bit nerdy, but it's actually kind of fun to see your progress over time!

2.3 Identifying areas for potential savings

Now that we've got a clear picture of your spending and a budget in place, it's time for the fun part – finding areas where you can save! This is where you get to flex your creative muscles and start thinking outside the box.

First, take a look at your expense tracking and your new budget. Where are the big chunks of spending? These are often the best places to start looking for savings because even small changes can have a big impact. Here are some common areas where people often find they can cut back:

1. Housing: This is usually the biggest expense for most people. Could you negotiate your rent? Refinance your mortgage? Get a roommate? If you're really looking to make a big change, would downsizing be an option?

2. Transportation: How much are you spending on your car? Between payments, insurance, gas, and maintenance, it adds up fast. Could you carpool, use public transportation, or bike more often? If you're a two-car household, could you get by with just one?

3. Food: This is a big one for a lot of people. How often are you eating

out or ordering in? Could your meal prep more? Shop with a list to avoid impulse buys? Buy generic instead of name-brand?

4. Utilities: There are often easy wins here. Could you adjust your thermostat a few degrees? Switch to LED bulbs? Take shorter showers?

5. Subscriptions and memberships: We often sign up for things and forget about them. Go through your subscriptions – do you really use that gym membership? All those streaming services? That magazine subscription?

6. Insurance: When was the last time you shopped around for better rates on your car or home insurance? You might be surprised at how much you could save.

7. Debt: High-interest debt can be a real budget-killer. Could you consolidate or refinance to get a lower interest rate?

Now, I want to emphasize something here: the goal isn't to cut out everything you enjoy. That's not sustainable, and frankly, it's no way to live. The idea is to cut back on the things that don't bring you much joy or value, so you can spend on the things that do.

For example, I realized I was spending a lot on cable TV, but I really only watched a few shows. I cut the cord and switched to a couple of streaming services, and now I'm saving over $100 a month. That's money I can put towards travel, which is way more important to me than having 500 channels I never watch.

Another area where I found surprising savings was in my grocery bill. I started meal planning and shopping with a list, and it made a huge difference. Not only did I save money, but I also reduced my food waste, which made me feel good about doing something for the environment too.

One strategy that can be really effective is the "painless saving" approach. Look for ways to save that you'll barely notice. For example:

- Call your cell phone provider and ask if there's a better plan for your usage. You might be able to save $10 or $20 a month without changing your habits at all.

- Set up automatic transfers to your savings account on payday. Start small – even $20 a paycheck adds up over time, and you'll adjust to living on slightly less.

- Use cashback apps or credit cards for purchases you're making

anyway. Just be sure to pay off
the credit card in full each month!

Saving money doesn't have to mean living like a monk. It's about being intentional with your spending and finding creative ways to reduce costs without sacrificing your quality of life.

As you're looking for areas to save, don't forget to think long-term too. Sometimes spending a bit more upfront can lead to big savings down the line. For example, investing in a good quality coat that'll last for years instead of buying a cheap one every winter. Or learning to do some basic home or car maintenance yourself instead of always calling in a pro.

One thing that really helped me was to make saving into a game. I started challenging myself to "no-spend days" where I'd go a whole day without spending any money. Or I'd see how long I could go without buying any new clothes. It turned what could have felt like deprivation into a fun challenge.

Another tip: don't try to change everything at once. Pick one or two areas to focus on at first. Maybe this month you work on reducing your grocery bill, and next month you tackle your entertainment spending. Small, consistent changes add up to big results over time.

And hey, don't forget to celebrate your wins! Did you come in under budget this month? Awesome! Maybe use a small portion of those savings to treat yourself to something you enjoy. It's important to reward yourself for your efforts – it helps keep you motivated for the long haul.

This is a process. You're not going to get it perfect right away, and that's okay. There will be months where unexpected expenses pop up, or where you go over budget in some categories. That's life! The important thing is to keep tracking, keep adjusting, and keep moving forward.

Assessing your financial situation and looking for ways to save is like starting a fitness routine. At first, it might feel uncomfortable or even a bit painful. You might be confronted with some hard truths about your spending habits. But stick with it, and I promise it gets easier. You'll start to feel more in control of your money, less stressed about your finances, and excited about the possibilities that open up when you're being smart with your cash.

There you have it – a deep dive into assessing your financial situation, creating a budget, and finding areas to save. It might seem like a lot, but take it one step at a time. Start by tracking your expenses, then move on to creating a budget, and then look for those areas to save. Before you know it, you'll be a pro at managing your money, and you'll have taken a huge step towards living that frugal (but fabulous) life.

The goal here isn't to become a penny-pinching miser. It's about aligning your spending with your values, so you can live your best life without constantly stressing about money. You've got this!

CHAPTER 3

Reducing Housing Costs

3.1 Choosing affordable housing options

First things first, let's talk about choosing where to live. Now, I know what you're thinking - "Choose? Ha! As if I have a choice in this crazy housing market!"
But hear me out. There are usually more options than you might think, even if some of them require a bit of creative thinking.

If you're renting, one of the most obvious ways to save is to downsize. I know, I know, nobody likes the idea of moving to a smaller place. But ask yourself - do you really need that extra bedroom that's just become a storage room for all the stuff you never use? Could you make do with a smaller living room if it meant having an extra couple hundred bucks in your pocket each month? Sometimes, less really is more.

Consider moving to a less trendy neighborhood. Sure, it's nice to be in the heart of all the action, but is it worth the premium you're paying? Often, you can find similar amenities just a few blocks or a short bus ride away, for a fraction of the cost. Plus, you might discover some hidden gems in your new neighborhood that you never knew existed.

Now, here's an idea that might make some of you cringe, but stick with me - what about getting a roommate? I can already hear the collective groan, but seriously, splitting rent and utilities can make a massive difference to your bottom line. And it doesn't have to be a nightmare scenario of dirty dishes and loud music at 2 AM. There are plenty of respectful, clean, quiet roommates out there. You just need to be picky and set clear ground rules from the start.

If you're in a position to buy rather than rent, consider looking at fixer-uppers. Yes, they require more work upfront, but you can often get a great deal on a house that just needs a little TLC. Plus, you get to customize it exactly how you want. Just make sure you're realistic about the amount of work required and get a thorough inspection before committing.

Another option that's gaining popularity is tiny houses. Now, I'm not saying you need to cram your whole life into 200 square feet (unless that appeals to you), but there are plenty of smaller, more efficient home designs out there that can save you a ton on both upfront costs and ongoing expenses.

Don't be afraid to negotiate. Whether you're renting or buying, there's often more wiggle room in the price than you might think. The worst they can say is no, right? I once managed to get my landlord to knock $50 off my monthly rent just by asking and pointing out that

I'd been a reliable tenant for years. That's $600 a year for a five-minute conversation!

3.2 Energy-saving tips for the home

Okay, so now that we've got you into a more affordable living situation, let's talk about how to keep those ongoing costs down. One of the biggest culprits when it comes to housing expenses? Energy costs. But fear not, I've got some tips that'll have you feeling like a sustainability superhero while also saving you some cash.

First up, let's talk about that thermostat. I know, it's tempting to crank up the heat in winter and blast the AC in summer, but each degree can make a big difference to your energy bill. Try setting your thermostat a little lower in winter and a little higher in summer. Put on a cozy sweater when it's cold, and embrace the beauty of a good fan when it's hot. You'd be surprised how quickly you adapt.

Speaking of fans, they're not just for summer. In winter, switch your ceiling fans to rotate clockwise. This pushes warm air down from the ceiling, helping to distribute heat more evenly and potentially allowing you to lower your thermostat even more.

Next, let's shine a light on your lighting situation. If you haven't already, it's time to make the switch to LED bulbs. Yes, they cost more upfront, but they use way less energy and last much longer than traditional bulbs. Trust me, your future self (and your wallet) will thank you.

Now, let's talk about those energy vampires lurking in your home. No, not actual vampires (though that would be an interesting problem to have). I'm talking about all those electronics and appliances that suck power even when they're not in use. Things like your TV, computer, and even your coffee maker can draw power when they're in standby mode. The solution? Plug them into power strips that you can easily switch off when not in use.

Here's a tip that's often overlooked: check your water heater settings. Many water heaters are set higher than necessary. Lowering the temperature to around 120°F (about 49°C) can save you money without you noticing any difference in your shower.

Don't underestimate the power of good old-fashioned window coverings. Keep your blinds or curtains closed during the hottest parts of the day in summer to keep your home cooler, and open them to let in warming sunlight during winter days.

3.3 DIY home maintenance and repairs

Alright, now we're getting to the fun part (or the scary part, depending on how you feel about DIY). Learning to do some basic home maintenance and repairs yourself can save you a ton of money in the long run. Plus, there's something really satisfying about fixing something with your own two hands.

Now, I'm not saying you should rewire your whole house or try to fix a major plumbing disaster. There are definitely times when you need to call in the pros. But there are plenty of smaller tasks that most of us can handle with a bit of research and patience.

Let's start with something simple: changing your air filters. This is an easy task that can make a big difference to your energy bills and the air quality in your home. Most filters should be changed every 1-3 months, depending on the type. Set a reminder on your phone so you don't forget.

Another easy win is caulking. Check around your windows and doors for any gaps or cracks, and seal them up with some caulk. This can help keep drafts out and your heated or cooled air in, saving you money on energy costs. Plus, it's oddly satisfying – like drawing with a giant, sticky pen.

Feel a draft coming from under your door? No problem! You can make a simple draft stopper with a pool noodle and some fabric. Just cut the pool noodle to size, wrap it in fabric, and voila! You've got yourself a cute and functional draft stopper.

Now, let's talk about painting. Hiring someone to paint your home can be expensive, but it's a task that most of us can handle ourselves with a bit of patience and some YouTube tutorials.

Just make sure you prep properly – that's the key to a professional-looking finish.

For the slightly more adventurous DIYers out there, learning to fix a leaky faucet can save you a costly plumber's visit. It's often just a matter of replacing a washer or O-ring, which is much easier than it sounds. Just remember to turn off the water supply before you start!

One of my favorite money-saving DIY tricks is making my own cleaning products. Not only is it cheaper, but it's also better for the environment. A simple mix of vinegar and water works wonders on windows and mirrors, and baking soda is great for scrubbing sinks and tubs.

Now, here's the thing about DIY – it's important to know your limits. If you're not sure you can handle a task safely, or if it involves major systems like electricity or gas, it's best to call in a professional. The money you save isn't worth risking your safety or causing more expensive damage.

But for those tasks you can handle, the internet is your friend. There are tons of great tutorials out there for just about any home repair or maintenance task you can think of. Just be sure to cross-reference a few different sources to make sure you're getting reliable information.

Invest in some basic tools. You don't need a fully stocked workshop, but having things like a good set of screwdrivers, a hammer, pliers, and a drill can set you up to handle a wide range of tasks. And don't be afraid to borrow or rent tools for one-off jobs. No need to buy a tile cutter if you're only retiling your bathroom once!

So there you have it – a whole bunch of ways to reduce your housing costs. From choosing more affordable living situations to saving energy and tackling some DIY, there are plenty of options to keep more money in your pocket without sacrificing the comfort of your home.

Start small, maybe with changing those air filters or sealing up some drafts. As you get more comfortable, you can take on bigger projects. Before you know it, you'll be amazed at how much you're saving and how handy you've become.

And hey, even if your DIY project doesn't turn out perfect, that's okay. My first attempt at painting a room looked like a kindergarten art project gone wrong. But you know what? I learned from it, and the next time was much better. Plus, I saved a bunch of money and had some laughs along the way. And isn't that what frugal living is all about? Saving money, learning new skills, and maybe having a bit of fun in the process. So go on, grab that caulking gun and show your home who's boss!

CHAPTER 4

Saving on Food and Groceries

4.1 Meal planning and bulk cooking

Okay, first things first: meal planning. I know, I know, it sounds about as exciting as watching paint dry. But trust me, this is a game-changer when it comes to saving money on food. Plus, it takes away that daily stress of "What the heck am I going to make for dinner?"

Here's how I do it: Every weekend, I sit down with a cup of coffee and plan out my meals for the week. I check what I already have in the fridge and pantry, look at what's on sale at the grocery store, and then make my plan. It doesn't have to be anything fancy - just a simple list of what you'll eat each day.

The key here is to be realistic. If you know you're going to be working late on Wednesday, don't plan an elaborate three-course meal. Maybe that's your leftovers night or your "breakfast for dinner" night. (Pancakes at 8 PM? Yes, please!)

Once you've got your meal plan, make a grocery list based on what you need for those meals. And here's the important part: stick to that list when you go shopping. It's amazing how much you can save just by avoiding those impulse buys. (I'm looking at you, fancy cheese section.)

Now, let's talk about bulk cooking. This is my secret weapon for busy weeks. The idea is simple: cook a big batch of something on the weekend, and then eat it throughout the week. It could be a big pot of chili, a lasagna, or even just cooking up a bunch of chicken breasts that you can use in different meals.

For example, I might cook a big batch of rice and a tray of roasted vegetables on Sunday. Then during the week, I can quickly throw together stir-fries, grain bowls, or even burritos. It's like having your own homemade "ready meals," but way cheaper and healthier than the store-bought versions.

One of my favorite bulk cooking hacks is what I call the "rotisserie chicken transformation." I'll buy a rotisserie chicken (often on sale at the end of the day), and then use it for multiple meals. Night one might be simple roast chicken with veggies. Night two could be chicken tacos. Then I'll use the leftover meat in a salad or sandwich, and finally boil the bones for a homemade chicken stock. That's four meals from one chicken!

4.2 Smart grocery shopping strategies

Alright, now that we've got our meal plan and our grocery list, let's talk about how to be a savvy shopper. First up: sales and coupons. Now, I'm not talking about extreme couponing where you end up with a basement full of mustard. But keeping an eye on sales and using coupons for things you actually need can lead to some serious savings.

Most grocery stores have apps now where you can see what's on sale and clip digital coupons. Take a few minutes to browse through these before you shop. And don't be afraid to stock up on non-perishables when they're on sale. Just make sure you'll actually use them before they expire.

Next tip: shop seasonally. Fruits and veggies are usually cheapest when they're in season. Plus, they taste better too! In the summer, load up on berries and tomatoes. In the fall, go crazy with apples and squash. Your taste buds and your wallet will thank you.

Here's a strategy that's saved me a ton: shop the perimeter of the store first. That's usually where you'll find the fresh produce, meat, and dairy. Fill your cart with these essentials before hitting the inner aisles. Those middle aisles are where all the processed, packaged (and often more expensive) foods live. By the time you get there, your cart should already be pretty full of healthy, whole foods.

Don't be afraid to try store brands, either. Often, they're made by the same manufacturers as the name brands, just with different packaging. Start with simple things like flour, sugar, or canned vegetables. If you like them, you can branch out to other products. I've found some store brand items that I actually prefer to the name brands!

Another money-saving hack: buy whole foods rather than pre-prepared ones. Sure, those pre-cut fruit platters look convenient, but you're paying a premium for someone else to do the chopping. Buying a whole pineapple and cutting it yourself is way cheaper (and kind of fun, if you ask me).

Oh, and here's a tip that might sound obvious but is easy to forget: don't shop hungry! Everything looks good when you're starving, and you'll end up buying way more than you need. Have a snack before you go, and you'll be much more likely to stick to your list.

Lastly, consider checking out discount grocery stores or ethnic markets. You can often find great deals on staples like rice, beans, and spices at these places. Plus, you might discover some new favorite foods in the process!

4.3 Growing your own food

Okay, now we're getting to my favorite part: growing your own food. There's something incredibly satisfying about eating something you've grown yourself. Plus, it's a great way to save money on produce. And before you say, "But I don't have a green thumb!" or "I live in an apartment!", hear me out. There are options for everyone.

If you've got a yard, starting a vegetable garden can be a great way to save money on produce. Start small with a few easy-to-grow veggies like tomatoes, zucchini, or leafy greens. You don't need a huge plot - even a small raised bed can produce a surprising amount of food.

No yard? No problem! Container gardening is your friend. You can grow herbs on your windowsill, cherry tomatoes on your balcony, or even lettuce in a hanging basket. I once grew a pretty impressive crop of chili peppers on my fire escape (just make sure this is allowed in your building before you try it!).

For those of you thinking, "But I kill every plant I touch!", let me introduce you to the wonders of herb gardening. Herbs are pretty forgiving, and even if you only keep them alive for a few weeks, you'll still save money compared to buying those little plastic packs at the grocery store. Plus, nothing beats the taste of fresh basil or cilantro in your cooking.

If you're feeling ambitious, you could look into community gardens in your area. These are shared spaces where you can rent a small plot to grow your own vegetables. It's a great way to get some gardening space if you don't have your own, plus you get to meet other gardeners and swap tips (and probably some zucchini - everyone always has too much zucchini).

For those in colder climates, don't think your growing season is limited to the summer. You can start seeds indoors in the late winter/early spring to get a jump on the season. And cold-hardy crops like kale and Brussels sprouts can often survive well into the fall or even winter.

One of my favorite money-saving garden hacks is regrowth. Did you know you can regrow certain vegetables from kitchen scraps? Green onions, lettuce, and celery are great for this. Just put the root end in a shallow dish of water, and watch them grow. It's like getting free veggies!

If you're new to gardening, start small and don't get discouraged if things don't work out perfectly the first time. Gardening is a learning process, and even experienced gardeners have crops fail sometimes. The key is to keep trying. And hey, even if you only end up with one tomato, that's still one tomato you didn't have to buy!

Now, let's talk about preserving your harvest. If you end up with more produce than you can eat (looking at you again, zucchini), learning some basic preservation techniques can help you enjoy your homegrown goodies all year round. Freezing is the easiest - most vegetables can be blanched and frozen for later use. Or you could try your hand at canning or making jams. Just be sure to follow proper food safety guidelines.

save your seeds! Many vegetables produce seeds that you can save and plant the next year. This not only saves you money on buying new seeds, but over time, you'll develop plants that are perfectly adapted to your specific growing conditions.

So, there you have it - a whole bunch of ways to save money on food and groceries. From meal planning and smart shopping to growing your own herbs and veggies, there are tons of options to keep your belly full and your wallet happy.

Maybe start with meal planning this week, try out a new grocery shopping strategy next week, and plant some herbs in a few weeks. Small changes add up over time, and before you know it, you'll be a pro at saving money on food.

And hey, don't forget to have some fun with it! Try out new recipes with your bulk-cooked meals. Turn grocery shopping into a game where you try to beat your "high score" for savings. Name the plants in your herb garden (am I the only one who does that?).

At the end of the day, food is more than just fuel - it's a source of joy, creativity, and connection. So while we're trying to save money, let's not forget to enjoy the process. Who knows? You might just discover a new favorite recipe, find a hidden talent for gardening, or become the king or queen of leftover makeovers. Happy eating, and happy saving!

CHAPTER 5

Minimizing Utility Costs

5.1 Reducing electricity usage

First up, let's tackle the electricity bill.
You know, that one that makes you
wonder if you've been secretly powering
a small city from your living room. The
good news is, there are tons of ways to
cut down on your electricity usage
without sitting in the dark or giving up
your favorite gadgets.

Let's start with the low-hanging fruit:
lighting. If you haven't already made the
switch to LED bulbs, what are you
waiting for? I know, I know, they're
more expensive upfront. But trust me,
these little guys will save you a bundle in
the long run. They use way less energy
and last forever. I swear I've had the
same LED bulb in my desk lamp since

college, and I'm not telling you how long ago that was!

Next up, let's talk about those energy vampires lurking in your home. No, I'm not talking about your teenager who leaves every light on (though that's a problem too). I'm talking about all those devices that suck power even when they're "off." Your TV, computer, phone charger – they're all guilty. The solution? Plug them into power strips that you can easily switch off when you're not using them. It's like garlic for energy vampires!

Now, let's address the elephant in the room: heating and cooling. This is usually the biggest energy hog in most homes. The easiest way to save? Adjust your thermostat. In winter, try setting it a few degrees cooler and bundling up in a cozy sweater. In summer, set it a bit higher and embrace the joy of a good ceiling fan. Speaking of fans, did you know that most ceiling fans have a switch to change the direction they spin?

In summer, you want them spinning counterclockwise to create a cool breeze. In winter, switch them to clockwise to help distribute warm air that rises to the ceiling. Mind-blowing, right?

Here's a fun one: use your appliances strategically. Run your dishwasher and washing machine only when they're full. Use cold water for laundry when possible (bonus: your clothes will last longer too). And try to avoid using your oven on hot summer days – it's a great excuse for a barbecue!

Oh, and let's not forget about natural light. Open those curtains and let the sun shine in! Not only will it save on lighting costs, but it's also a great mood booster. Just be sure to close them when the sun is directly hitting your windows in summer to keep the heat out.

consider a programmable or smart thermostat. These nifty devices can automatically adjust your home's temperature based on your schedule. Coming home from work at 6 PM every day? Set it to start cooling or heating shortly before you arrive. No need to keep an empty house comfortable all day!

5.2 Water conservation techniques

Alright, now let's talk about water. You know, that stuff that covers most of our planet but somehow still costs us money every month. The good news is, there are plenty of ways to reduce your water usage without turning your home into a desert.

First up, let's address the bathroom. This is where a lot of water waste happens. If you have an older toilet, consider replacing it with a low-flow model. Can't swing a new toilet right now? No problem. Put a filled water bottle in your tank to displace some water and reduce the amount used per flush. Just make sure it doesn't interfere with the flushing mechanism.

Now, let's talk about your shower. I know, I know, a long hot shower feels amazing. But it's also a huge water waster. Try cutting your shower time by just a couple of minutes. You'd be amazed at how much water this saves over time. And if you're feeling really ambitious, consider installing a low-flow showerhead. Modern ones are actually pretty great – you'll still get good water pressure, I promise!

Here's a fun fact: a running faucet wastes about 2 gallons per minute. So turn off the tap while you're brushing your teeth or shaving. It's a small change that can make a big difference. And while we're talking about faucets, check yours for leaks. Even a small drip can waste a lot of water over time. Fixing a leaky faucet is usually a pretty easy DIY job – there are tons of tutorials online.

Moving on to the kitchen: when washing dishes by hand, don't let the water run continuously. Fill up one side of the sink (or a large bowl) with soapy water for washing, and the other side with clean water for rinsing. And if you have a dishwasher, use it! Modern dishwashers actually use less water than washing by hand, as long as you run full loads.

Now, let's step outside. If you have a yard or garden, water is probably a big part of your usage. The key here is to water smart. Water early in the morning or late in the evening when it's cooler to reduce evaporation. Use mulch around your plants to help retain moisture. And if you're feeling fancy, consider installing a rain barrel to collect rainwater for your garden. It's like free water from the sky!

Oh, and here's a weird tip that actually works: put a few drops of food coloring in your toilet tank. If the color shows up in the bowl without flushing, you've got a leak that needs fixing. It's like a fun science experiment that can save you money!

5.3 Negotiating better rates with service providers

Okay, now we're getting into the part that makes a lot of people uncomfortable: negotiating. I get it, nobody likes confrontation. But remember, these companies want to keep you as a customer. You have more power than you think!

First things first: do your homework. Research what other providers in your area are offering. Knowledge is power, my friends. Once you're armed with information, give your current provider a call. Be polite but firm. Let them know you've been shopping around and you've found better rates elsewhere. Often, they'll offer you a better deal to keep your business.

If they won't budge on the price, ask if there are any promotions or discounts you might be eligible for. Sometimes there are special rates for students, seniors, or even just long-time customers that aren't advertised. It never hurts to ask!

Don't be afraid to mention any issues you've had with their service. If you've had frequent outages or billing problems, bring these up. Companies often have retention departments specifically tasked with keeping customers happy. They may offer you a discount or credit to make up for past issues.

Now, here's a pro tip: timing is everything. Try calling near the end of the month or quarter. Companies often have quotas to meet, and representatives might be more willing to cut you a deal to hit their targets.

If you're not having any luck on the phone, try reaching out via social media.

Some companies have dedicated customer service teams monitoring their social channels, and they're often empowered to offer special deals to keep customers happy (and prevent public complaints).

You don't have to limit yourself to just your current provider. Get quotes from other companies in your area. Sometimes the threat of switching is enough to get your current provider to offer a better deal. And if it's not, well, maybe it is time to switch!

One more thing: bundle, bundle, bundle! Many companies offer discounts if you get multiple services from them. If you're getting your internet, TV, and phone service from different providers, see if you can save by bundling them together.

Now, I know what some of you are thinking: "But I live in an area with only one option for [insert utility here]." I feel you. In these cases, your options are more limited, but you're not totally powerless. Look into energy-saving programs or rebates offered by your utility company. Many have programs that can help you save money by using less energy or water.

And hey, if all else fails, consider reducing your usage of that particular utility. Maybe it's time to cut the cord on cable TV and switch to streaming. Or maybe you can downgrade your internet speed if you're not using all that bandwidth. Sometimes the best way to save is simply to use less.

So, there you have it – a whole bunch of ways to minimize your utility costs. From simple changes like switching to LED bulbs and taking shorter showers, to more involved strategies like negotiating with your service providers, there are plenty of options to keep more money in your pocket.

Start with one or two easy changes and work your way up. Every little bit helps, and those savings will add up over time. Before you know it, you'll be looking at your utility bills with a smile instead of a grimace.

And hey, don't forget to pat yourself on the back for taking these steps. You're not just saving money – you're also helping the environment by using fewer resources. It's a win-win!

So go forth and conquer those utility bills! Turn off those lights, fix those leaky faucets, and don't be afraid to make that phone call to your service provider. You've got this! And who knows? Maybe you'll even have fun with it. There's a certain thrill in seeing how low you can get those bills. It's like a game, but instead of points, you win money. Now that's my kind of game!

CHAPTER 6

Frugal Fashion and Personal Care

6.1 Building a minimalist wardrobe

First things first, let's talk about building a minimalist wardrobe. Now, I know the word "minimalist" might conjure up images of stark white rooms and people wearing nothing but black turtlenecks. But that's not what we're going for here (unless that's your jam, in which case, rock on!). What we're talking about is creating a wardrobe that's versatile, functional, and filled with pieces you actually love and wear.

The key to a minimalist wardrobe is quality over quantity. I know, I know, it's tempting to load up on cheap fast fashion pieces. But trust me, in the long run, you'll save money (and look better) by investing in fewer, higher-quality items that will last longer and stay in style.

Start by taking inventory of what you already have. Be honest with yourself – what do you actually wear? What makes you feel great when you put it on? These are the pieces you want to keep. Everything else? It might be time to say goodbye (don't worry, we'll talk about what to do with those clothes later).

Now, let's talk about the foundation of your wardrobe – the basics. These are the pieces that you can mix and match to create a ton of different outfits. I'm talking about things like:

- A good pair of jeans that fit you perfectly

- A white t-shirt (or whatever neutral color you prefer)

- A versatile blazer

- A little black dress (or a suit, depending on your style and needs)

- A pair of well-fitting black pants

- A few basic tops in colors that work well together

The exact items will depend on your personal style and lifestyle, but the idea is to have pieces that can be dressed up or down and mixed and matched easily.

Here's a pro tip: stick to a color palette. This doesn't mean everything has to be black and white (unless that's your thing). But choosing colors that work well together will make it much easier to create outfits. Plus, it'll help you avoid those "I have nothing to wear" moments when you're staring at a closet full of clothes.

Now, I'm not saying you can't have fun with your wardrobe. By all means, throw in some statement pieces or trendy items if that's what you love. The key is to make sure these pieces still work with the rest of your wardrobe. And maybe limit yourself to one or two trend pieces per season, rather than trying to keep up with every new fad.

The goal of a minimalist wardrobe isn't to make your life boring or to never buy new clothes. It's about being intentional with your choices, investing in pieces you truly love, and creating a wardrobe that makes getting dressed easier and more enjoyable. Plus, when you're not constantly buying new clothes, you'll have more money for other things – like that vacation you've been dreaming about!

6.2 Thrift shopping and clothes swapping

Alright, now let's talk about one of my favorite ways to refresh my wardrobe without spending a fortune: thrift shopping! I swear, there's nothing quite like the thrill of finding an amazing piece for a fraction of its original price. It's like a treasure hunt, but instead of gold, you're finding vintage Levi's and designer dresses.

If you've never been thrift shopping before, here are a few tips to get you started:

1. Be patient. You might not find something amazing every time, and that's okay. The best finds often come when you least expect them.

2. Check for quality. Just because something's cheap doesn't mean it's a good deal if it's falling apart. Look for well-made pieces that will last.

3. Try things on. Sizes can be wonky in thrift stores, especially with vintage pieces. Don't be afraid to

try on things that might not be your usual size.

4. Think creatively. That oversized men's shirt? It could be a cute dress with a belt. Those jeans that are too long? Hem them or cuff them for a new look.

5. Know when to walk away. It's easy to get carried away with the low prices, but only buy things you'll actually wear.

Now, if you're worried about the "ick" factor of secondhand clothes, don't be. Most thrift stores are pretty picky about what they accept, and a good wash will take care of any concerns. Plus, think about how many people have tried on that "new" shirt at the department store!

Another great way to refresh your wardrobe for free is through clothes swapping. Get a group of friends together, have everyone bring clothes they no longer want, and swap away! It's a fun way to spend an afternoon, and you might come away with some great new (to you) pieces. Plus, it's a great excuse to hang out with your friends and maybe enjoy a glass of wine or two.

If you don't have friends who are into swapping (or if they're all a different size than you), look for clothing swap events in your area. Many cities have started organizing these, and they're a great way to meet new people while scoring some new clothes.

And hey, while we're talking about getting rid of clothes you no longer want, consider donating your old clothes to a local charity or thrift store. It's a great way to declutter your closet while potentially helping someone else find an awesome new outfit.

6.3 DIY beauty and personal care products

Okay, now let's talk about beauty and personal care. We all want to look our best, but man, those products can get expensive! The good news is, you can make a lot of great beauty and personal care products right at home, often with ingredients you already have in your kitchen.

Let's start with skincare. One of my favorite DIY face masks is just mashed up avocado. Seriously, that's it. Just mash up half an avocado and smear it on your face. Leave it for about 15 minutes, then rinse off. Your skin will feel amazing, and you can eat the other half of the avocado on some toast. Win-win!

Another great DIY skincare product is a sugar scrub. Mix equal parts sugar and oil (coconut oil, olive oil, whatever you have), and boom – you've got a body scrub that'll leave your skin feeling silky smooth. Add a few drops of essential oil if you want to get fancy.

Now, let's talk hair care. Have you ever tried an apple cider vinegar rinse? It sounds weird, I know, but it's amazing for your hair. Mix one part apple cider vinegar with three parts water, and use it as a final rinse after shampooing. It helps balance the pH of your scalp and leaves your hair super shiny. Just be warned – it doesn't smell great while you're doing it, but the smell disappears once your hair is dry.

For a deep conditioning treatment, try coconut oil. Just melt some in your hands and work it through your hair, focusing on the ends. Leave it on for an hour (or overnight if your hair is really dry), then shampoo out. Your hair will thank you!

Let's not forget about teeth! You can make your own toothpaste with just baking soda and coconut oil. Mix them into a paste, add a drop of peppermint essential oil if you want, and there you go. It's not as fancy as store-bought, but it gets the job done.

Now, I'm not saying you need to DIY everything. There are some things (like sunscreen, for example) that are best left to the professionals. But making some of your own products can save you a ton of money, and it's kind of fun too. Plus, you know exactly what's going into them – no weird chemicals or unpronounceable ingredients.

One word of caution: if you have sensitive skin or any allergies, be sure to patch test any new products (homemade or store-bought) before slathering them all over your face or body. The last thing you want is to save money on skincare only to end up needing to see a dermatologist!

And hey, while we're on the topic of beauty, let's talk about one of the best beauty treatments out there: sleep.

Seriously, getting enough sleep does wonders for your skin, hair, and overall appearance. And it's free! So make sure you're getting your beauty rest.

Now, I know what some of you might be thinking – "But what about makeup? I can't DIY that!" And you're right, for the most part. But you can be smart about your makeup purchases. Look for multi-use products (a lip color that can double as blush, for example). Buy drugstore dupes for high-end products (there are tons of YouTube videos comparing them). And remember, you don't need every new palette or lipstick that comes out. Stick to colors and products you know you'll actually use.

At the end of the day, being frugal with your fashion and personal care isn't about depriving yourself or never buying anything new. It's about being intentional with your purchases, taking good care of what you have, and finding creative ways to look and feel your best without spending a fortune.

True style isn't about having the latest trend or the most expensive products. It's about feeling confident and comfortable in your own skin. And that, my friend, is something you can't buy at any price.

So go forth and rock your minimalist wardrobe, score those thrift store finds, and whip up some DIY beauty treatments. You'll look fabulous, feel great, and have some extra cash in your pocket. And who knows? You might even have some fun along the way. After all, there's nothing more stylish than being smart with your money!

CHAPTER 7

Entertainment and Leisure on a Budget

7.1 Free and low-cost activities

Okay, let's kick things off with everyone's favorite price: free! Yep, you heard that right. There are tons of ways to have a blast without spending a dime. Let's explore some options, shall we?

First up, let's talk about the great outdoors. Mother Nature is basically the world's biggest free theme park, and she's open 24/7. Hiking is a fantastic way to get some exercise, enjoy beautiful scenery, and maybe even have a picnic with a view. Just grab some comfy shoes, pack a sandwich, and hit the trails. Don't have any hiking spots nearby? No problem! Even a walk in your local park can be a great way to spend an afternoon.

Bring a frisbee or a soccer ball, and suddenly you've got yourself a fun, active day out.

Now, if you're more of an indoor person (no judgment here, I get it), how about starting a game night tradition with your friends or family? Dust off those board games hiding in your closet, or break out a deck of cards. You'd be amazed at how much fun you can have with a simple game of Uno or Monopoly. Pro tip: make it a potluck where everyone brings a snack to share. Boom! Cheap entertainment and dinner sorted.

Here's another idea: become a tourist in your own city. I bet there are tons of cool spots in your area that you've never checked out. Maybe there's a quirky statue downtown, or a historical landmark you've always driven past but never visited. Make a list of interesting places in your area and start exploring. It's like a treasure hunt, but instead of gold, you find cool Instagram photo ops.

Speaking of photo ops, how about a photography challenge? You don't need a fancy camera – your smartphone will do just fine. Pick a theme (like "things that are red" or "interesting shadows") and go on a photo walk around your neighborhood. It's a great way to see familiar surroundings with fresh eyes, and who knows? You might discover a hidden talent!

Now, let's talk about music. Free concerts are more common than you might think. Check your local community calendar for events in parks, libraries, or community centers. Many cities have summer concert series that are completely free. Pack a blanket, some snacks, and enjoy live music under the stars. It's like Coachella, but without the hefty price tag and questionable fashion choices.

Oh, and don't forget about free days at museums and galleries. Many cultural institutions offer free admission on certain days of the month. It's a great opportunity to soak up some culture without soaking your wallet. Even if art isn't usually your thing, give it a try. You might surprise yourself and discover a new interest.

For my fellow film buffs out there, keep an eye out for free movie screenings. Some parks do "Movies in the Park" events during summer. Universities often have film clubs that show movies for free or very cheap. And hey, if all else fails, host a movie night at home. Make some popcorn, dim the lights, and boom – you've got your own personal cinema.

Last but not least, volunteer! I know, I know, it sounds like work, not fun. But hear me out. Volunteering can be incredibly rewarding, and it often leads to new friendships and experiences. Plus, many volunteer opportunities involve fun events like community festivals or animal shelter play days. It's a win-win:

you're helping others and having a good time, all for free!

7.2 Using the library and community resources

Alright, now let's talk about one of the most underrated places for free entertainment: your local library. Trust me, libraries are way cooler than you might remember from your school days.

First off, books. Duh, right? But seriously, do you know how much money you can save by borrowing books instead of buying them? If you're a bookworm like me, it's probably enough to fund a small country. Plus, there's something magical about wandering through the stacks and discovering a new favorite author.

But here's the thing: libraries aren't just about books anymore. Many libraries now loan out movies, music, and even video games. It's like having a free Netflix subscription, but with a better selection of classics. Some libraries even have more unusual items you can borrow, like musical instruments, art prints, or even baking pans. It's worth checking out what your local library offers – you might be surprised!

Now, let's talk about events. Many libraries host a variety of free events and classes. We're talking book clubs, writing workshops, language exchange meetups, and even craft classes. I once attended a free origami workshop at my local library and left with a pretty sweet paper crane (okay, it was more like a paper blob, but I had fun making it).

For all you lifelong learners out there, libraries often provide free access to online courses and educational resources. Want to learn a new language? Check if your library offers free access to language learning software. Trying to boost your professional skills? Look into whether they provide access to LinkedIn Learning or similar platforms. It's like having a free pass to an online university.

Don't forget about the tech resources many libraries offer. Need to use a computer or print something? Most libraries have you covered. Some even have 3D printers or recording studios that patrons can use. It's a great way to try out new tech without investing in expensive equipment.

Now, let's expand our view beyond the library and look at other community resources. Community centers often offer free or low-cost classes and activities. You might find anything from yoga classes to cooking workshops to dance lessons. It's a great way to try new things without committing to an expensive gym membership or class series.

Check out your local parks and recreation department too. Many offer free or cheap fitness classes in parks during the summer. Some even organize community sports leagues that are way more affordable than private clubs.

If you're into gardening (or want to give it a try), look into whether your area has any community gardens. These are great for apartment dwellers who don't have their own outdoor space. Plus, you get the bonus of fresh veggies and new friends!

For my artsy friends out there, keep an eye out for community art projects. Many cities have programs where local artists lead free workshops or collaborative projects. It's a great way to get creative and maybe even contribute to a public art piece.

Lastly, don't underestimate the power of local online communities. Facebook groups, Next-door, or local subreddits can be great sources of information about free events and resources in your area. Plus, you might find groups organizing free meetups around shared interests, from book clubs to hiking groups to board game nights.

7.3 Frugal travel tips

Okay, I know what you're thinking. "Travel? On a budget? Yeah, right." But hold onto your hats, folks, because I'm about to blow your mind with some frugal travel tips that'll have you packing your bags without emptying your bank account.

First things first: flexibility is your best friend when it comes to budget travel. If you can be flexible with your dates and destinations, you can save a ton of money. Use tools like Skyscanner or Google Flights to check prices across a range of dates. Sometimes, flying on a

Tuesday instead of a Friday can save you hundreds of dollars.

Speaking of flights, let's talk about budget airlines. Yes, they might charge you for everything from choosing your seat to bringing a carry-on, but if you play by their rules, you can score some incredibly cheap flights. Just make sure to read the fine print and factor in any extra fees when comparing prices.

Now, here's a tip that's served me well: consider traveling in the off-season. Not only will flights and accommodations be cheaper, but you'll also avoid the crowds. Sure, you might need to pack a jacket instead of a swimsuit, but you'll get a more authentic experience of your destination without hordes of other tourists around.

Let's talk accommodations. Hotels are great, but they can eat up a huge chunk of your travel budget. Consider alternatives like hostels (they're not just for college kids anymore!), vacation rentals, or even couch surfing if you're feeling adventurous. I once stayed in a converted windmill in Amsterdam through Airbnb, and it was one of the coolest experiences of my life.

Here's a pro tip: look into house sitting or pet sitting. Websites like Trusted House sitter connect travelers with homeowners who need someone to watch their house (and often their pets) while they're away. You get free accommodation, they get peace of mind, and you might even get to cuddle with a cute dog or cat. Win-win-win!

Now, let's talk about getting around once you're at your destination. Public transportation is usually much cheaper than taxis or rental cars. Many cities offer tourist passes that give you unlimited use of public transit for a set number of days. Bonus: you'll feel like a local navigating the subway or bus system.

If public transit isn't an option, look into bike rentals. Many cities have bike-share programs that are super affordable. Plus, cycling is a great way to explore and work off all that delicious local food you'll be trying.

Speaking of food, eating out for every meal can quickly drain your travel budget. Hit up local markets or grocery stores and picnic in a park instead of a restaurant. Not only is it cheaper, but it's also a great way to people-watch and soak up the local atmosphere. When you do eat out, try to avoid the touristy areas – walk a few blocks away from the main attractions and you'll often find better food at better prices.

Here's a fun one: free walking tours. Many cities offer these, and they're a great way to get oriented and learn about the history and culture of your destination. While they're technically free, it's customary to tip your guide what you think the tour was worth.

For my culture vultures out there, many museums have free or discounted days. Do a little research before your trip to see if you can time your visits accordingly. Some cities even offer tourist cards that give you free entry to multiple attractions – these can be a great deal if you plan to do a lot of sightseeing.

Now, let's talk about one of my favorite travel hacks: airline rewards credit cards. If you're responsible with credit, these can be a great way to earn free flights or hotel stays. Just make sure you're not spending more just to earn points – that defeats the purpose of budget travel!

Here's a tip for my fellow remote workers: consider a workation. Combine work and vacation by staying somewhere with good WiFi for a few weeks. You can often find monthly discounts on vacation rentals, making it cheaper than a regular vacation. Plus, you get to really immerse yourself in a new place.

Don't underestimate the power of good old-fashioned camping. It's one of the cheapest ways to travel, especially if you already have gear. Many national and state parks have incredibly affordable camping fees, and you get to wake up surrounded by nature. Just remember to book in advance – the best spots often fill up quickly.

So, there you have it, folks – a whopping guide to entertainment and leisure on a budget. From free local activities to frugal world travels, there are so many ways to have fun without breaking the bank. Being on a budget doesn't mean you can't enjoy life. It just means you need to get a little creative and think outside the box.

The key is to focus on experiences rather than things. At the end of the day, it's the memories you make that matter, not how much you spent making them. Some of my favorite memories are from times when I had the least money – impromptu picnics in the park, game nights that turned into deep conversations until 3 AM, or that time I got gloriously lost in a new city and stumbled upon the most amazing little café.

So go forth and have fun, you frugal adventurers! Explore your local library, become a tourist in your own town, plan that budget trip you've been dreaming of.

Who knows? You might find that living on a budget actually enriches your life in ways you never expected. You might discover new hobbies, make new friends, or gain a deeper appreciation for the simple pleasures in life. And if nothing else, you'll have some great stories to tell – like that time you tried to make origami at the library and ended up with a paper blob instead of a crane. Hey, it's all part of the adventure!

So, are you ready to become a master of frugal fun? Trust me, your wallet will thank you, and your life will be all the richer for it. Now, if you'll excuse me, I've got a free concert in the park to attend. Happy budget adventuring, everyone!